WAY TO GO

34 Delightful ideas for ending it all with Elegance, Style and Class

Dress up like Cleopatra.
Order a reptile.

Be the first to traverse Antartica
with a sled dog team of Chihuahuas.

Bungie Jump
off the
Eiffel Tower

Uncover the tomb of Ramses II.
Prove that the Curse of the Pharaohs
is a lot of nonsense.

Take photos of the Piranha.

Plead with the Mafia to
give up their sinful ways.

Become Pedicurist to the
Circus Big Cats.

Smoke the world's longest cigarette.
You will be honored in the
Guiness Book of World Records.
Posthumously.

Have dolls made in your
likeness and throw a
Voodoo party.

Soak in a warm bath. Pet
your Yellow Electric Ducky.

Prove that you are the new Messiah. Walk on water.

Take a third-class bus from Mexico to Panama.

Vacation in Pamplona.

Go to a four-star restaurant in Paris. Order Poulet Roti au Beurre avec Pommes Frites Provençal. Request ketchup.

Do a Lady Godiva at the Southern Baptist Convention.

Sail around the world ...

in a bathtub.

Walk into a biker bar at
midnight. Pick a fight.

Make paintings showing the
various stages of starvation.

Take up Sumo Wrestling.

Watch all of the re-runs of
the Lawrence Welk Show.

Be stomped on by Spain's most famous Flamenco Dancer, Don Luis Ignazio Jose de La Fuerte y Hidalgo. Thursdays at 11 p.m.

Lay down five aces.
Claim the pot.

Go surfing on the Rocket Blast to Mars.
Hang nine dudes!

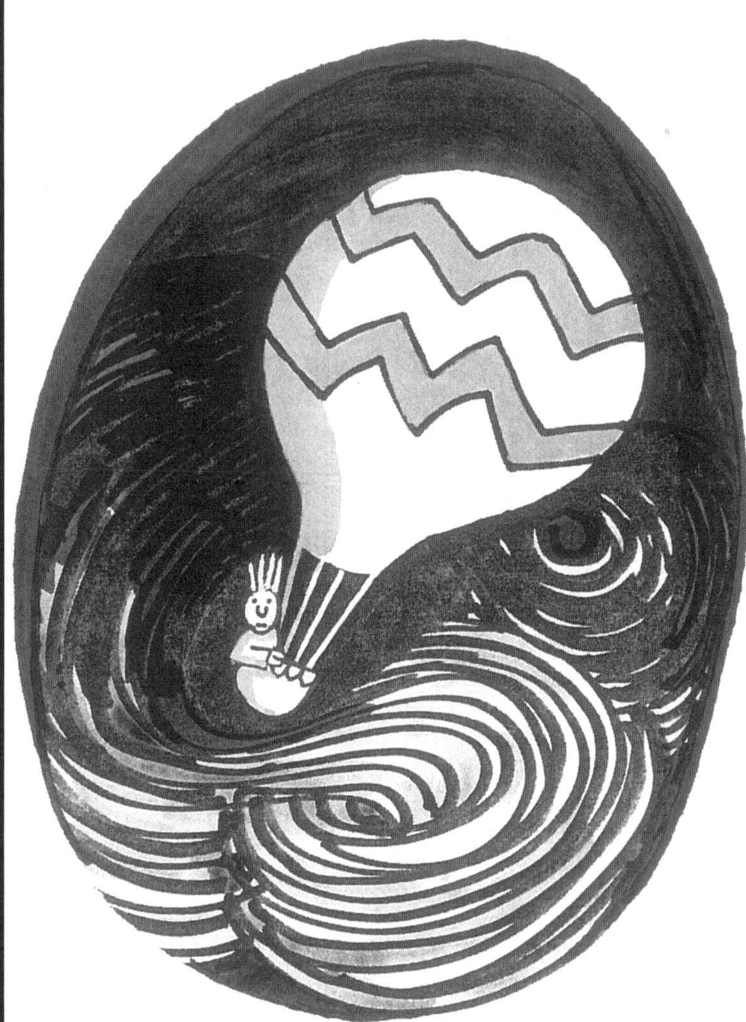

Track a Hurricane from a hot air balloon.

Be first in line for the Macys
day-after-Christmas sale.

Be wonderfully creative in
your home laboratory.

Write the world's longest suicide note. By the time you finish you will have died from natural causes.

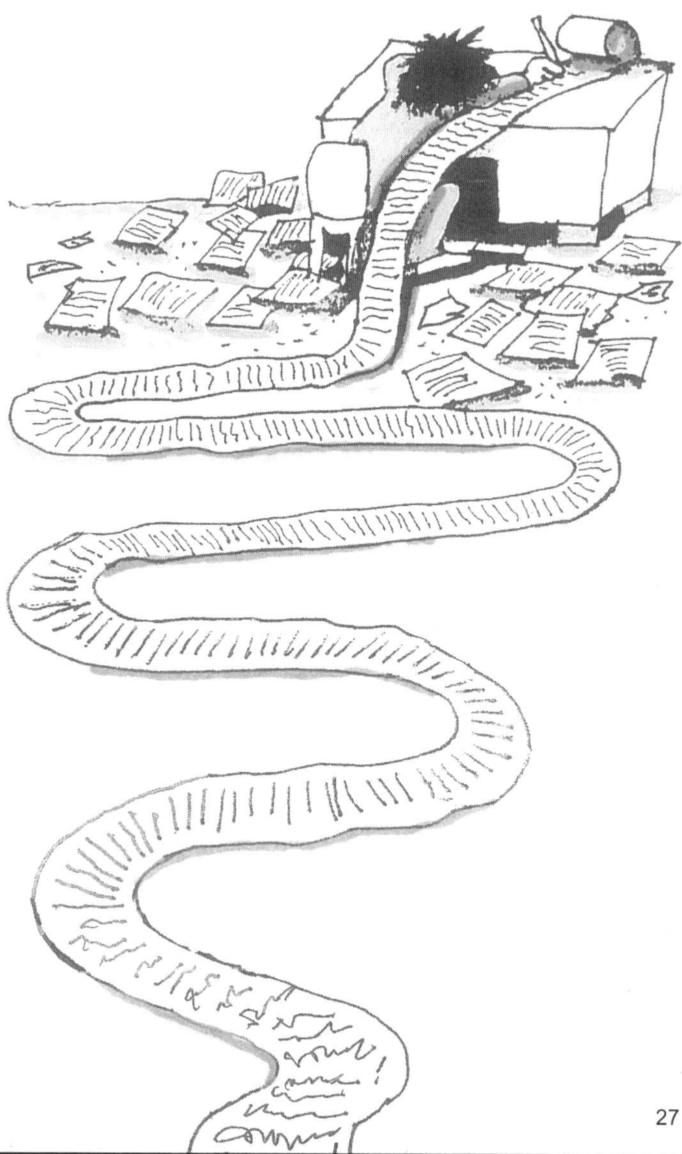

Dine with descendants of the Lucrezia Borgia Family.

Sneak into North Korea.
Tell Kim Jong Un he is a
fat, ugly little man.

Let cousin Charlie use you
for his newest experiment
with the Brain Enhancer.

Have fun with the fledglings
while waiting mother's return

Play kick-the-bucket off the top of Mt. Fuji.

Bring back wing-walking

AUTHOR'S NOTE

In 1995 I was diagnosed with prostate cancer.
Like many other men of that time, I panicked
and thought I would die in six months, maybe
a year. I thought the only way out for me was
to jump off the Golden Gate Bridge and end it
all. But being an old time gag writer and
cartoonist, the more I thought about it the more
I saw myself with a parachute, so that if I
changed my mind in mid-jump I could always
reverse the fall. Well, I made myself laugh.
And that was good. Very good.
  Then I drew some more gags about idiotic,
foolish, stupid, dumb ways to end it all, and
made myself laugh more. The end of this story
is that the laughter and the drawing awakened
me to the task at hand, mainly, getting help.
I did, it worked, and I'm still here.
  In 1996 I co-founded the Prostate Awareness
Foundation, a non-profit group that has helped
thousands of men find resources to survive and
thrive after diagnosis.
  www.prostateawarenessfoundation.org
WAY TO GO is a gathering of drawings I've
made over the past seventeen years.
  So, never underestimate the power of humor,
whether it comes from a cartoon, a joke, a song
or a funny face.
  It just might save your life.

ROBERT GUMPERTZ 100 SUMMIT AVENUE MILL VALLEY CA 94941
415.847.1336
www.gumpertzart.com
robert@gumpertzart.com

RESUME

Cartoons in Playboy, New York Times, Punch of London,
Penthouse, Paris Match and the San Francisco Chronicle

Author & Illustrator
THE INTERNATIONAL DOG Cartoon Book
Golden Press, New York

Author & Illustrator
PROFESSOR TWILL'S TRAVELS Children's Book
Houghton Mifflin Co., Boston

Creator & Designer *DREAM NOTEBOOK*
San Francisco Publishing

Author & Illustrator *FROM FIDDLETOWN TO TUBA CITY*
Cartoon Book Workman Publishing, New York

GALLERY SHOWS

2009 *Throckmorton Theatre Gallery* Mill Valley
Paintings and Monotypes

2008 *Himmelberger Gallery* San Francisco
Paintings, Drawings and Monotypes

2006 *Atelier Berner* Paris, France
Paintings

2002 *Blue Dome Gallery* Silver City, New Mexico
Paintings

1998 *Filbert Street Gallery* San Francisco
Paintings and drawings

Made in the USA
Monee, IL
07 July 2026

56552165R00022